M1 MACBOOK AIR USER GUIDE

A Complete Step By Step Instruction Manual for Beginners and seniors to Learn How to Use the New MacBook Air Using the M1 Chip Like A Pro With MacOS Tips And Tricks

BY

HERBERT A. CLARK

Table of Contents

INTRODUCTION

In November 2020, Apple introduced the new MacBook Air M1 chip which is Apple's first designed Arm-based chip. With the M1, the new Apple MacBook Air redefines MacBook Air as we know it. Yes, M1 chips are replacing older Intel chips and are getting faster and better.

The new MacBook Air has a higher performance than before and offers many more hours of battery life. The machine learning load is 9x faster, so the MacBook Air is faster in ML-based features such as face recognition and detection of object.

NEW FEATURES OF MACOS BIG SUR

macOS Big Sur, launched in 2020, is the latest version of macOS, released on November 12th.

New design

macOS Big Sur is the first major MacOS design since Mac OS X, where Apple introduces a new, modern, and familiar design that is focusing on content, consistency, and translucency.

The side and tool bars have been redesigned to better blend with each window, and the side panels are now fully functional. The toolbars at the top of application no longer has separated button, which provides a softer and more seamless version of the operating system.

Windows have a lighter design with softer edges that are rounded, and the icons in the app change slightly and have a color design. Apple has also designed icons for all local apps, giving them a uniform round shape and allowing them to disable wallpaper tinting to make it darker, in dark mode.

There are new logos everywhere on macOS Big Sur to explain where you click and what happens when you click on the toolbar, sidebar, and controls. Applications that share common tasks, such as checking mailboxes or calendars, share the same sign for consistency.

The design of the updated application can be seen in the refreshed Dock, which takes round corners like windows. The dock is clearer than before and has a more structured look that mixes with the desktop.

Menu bar and control center

At the top of the screen, the menu bar shines to better blend with the table and can be hidden just like a dock when not in use. It is easy to read the pull-down menu with more spaces between the lines.

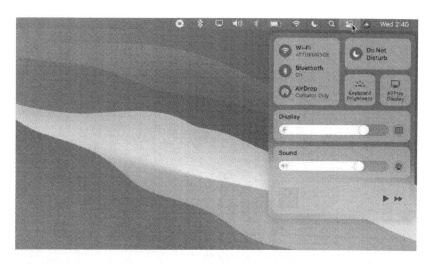

The menus and dropdown tables have been redesigned, and most importantly, the battery icon provides details about the amount of the remaining battery. The system preferences also has battery usage history, and for the first time, the macOS Big

Sur includes Optimized Battery Charging, which was included in macOS Catalina for the first time.

The menu bar is the home of a new control center for Mac that provides quick access control to keys such as, Wi-Fi, Bluetooth, sound, brightness, keyboard brightness, play now, Dark Mode, true tone, night shift, DND, and AirPlay. The control center is flexible, so you can place your most used features on your fingertips.

You can take the item you like on the menu and put it on top of the menu bar for quick access.

System Sounds

All the traditional Mac sounds have been updated and made **more pleasing to the ear**. Each sound consists of parts of the original sound, so they look familiar, but together they seem new.

Apple has also restarted the classic start-up chime, which was disconnected from the MacBook in 2016.

Notification center

The alert center has been updated and is now integrated with notifications with widgets to provide more information at a glance.

Notifications are integrated with the application and have additional related features, so you can do things like play a new podcast or reply to an email without opening the app. Press and hold a notification to get new options.

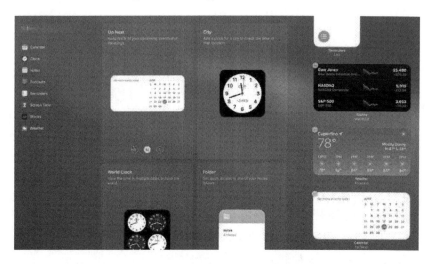

Widgets have been redesigned and look like widgets embedded in iOS 14, can be configured in three sizes, and have gallery of widgets to build what suits your needs. There are new widgets to work with programs like notes, screen time, podcasts, and more

The notification center's third-party tools are available on the Mac App Store.

Faster security and more reliable updates

macOS has a feature that allows Big Sur software updates to start in the background and then finish faster, so installing new software updates will not take long. Installing the macOS Big Sur is a requirement for this feature, so the first install of the macOS Big Sur takes a long time.

The program is used with new and cryptographically signed laws for Big Sur and adds protection against destructive tampering. macOS Big Sur also supports the backup of the APFS Time Machine, which allows you to use APFS disks to support your Mac in addition to HFS +.

Safari

Safari also has a new startup page that is personalized with wallpaper and includes options to add favorites, Frequently Accessed websites, Siri

Offers, Reading Lists, iCloud, tab, and a new Privacy reporting feature.

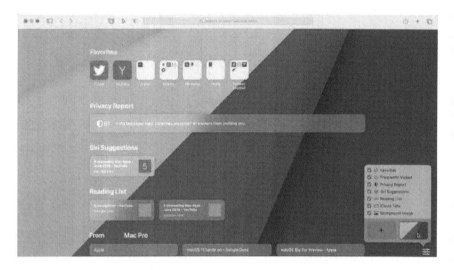

Safari is faster and more powerful than ever. Loading frequently visited websites is 50 percent faster than Chrome.

If you plan on changing your browser to take advantage of the new features in Big Sur, your history, bookmarks, and saved passwords can now be added to Safari from Chrome.

macOS Big Sur's Safari supports HDR video and works with 4K HDR and Dolby Vision content from Netflix and YouTube. Mac 2018 or later owners can watch 4K Netflix content on Safari while running Big Sur.

Privacy report

On the home page, the privacy report shows how many trackers have been prevented from getting hold of your profile, and you can see the trackers on the site page by clicking the shield icon next to the URL bar on the site

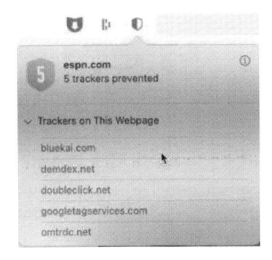

The Privacy Report provides a list of all trackers on the site and the number of blocked trackers, which prevents pages from being saved in your browsing habits. You can see up to how many trackers have been blocked in the 30 days from the Privacy report menu bar.

Tabs

The tabs in Safari has been redesigned and the tabs are more visible, with a new hover view that allows you to navigate through a tab to preview the page. There are also icons in the tabs, so you can see what to do at a glance.

Extensions

The Mac App Store has categories for extensions and has added support for the Web Extensions API, which allows you to modify extensions created for other browsers such as Apple, Chrome, and Edge. and Firefox, as a feature that works with Safari, which increases the number of extensions available to Safari users.

With added emphasis on expansion, Apple has added special privacy security suggestions. You can choose which pages the extension can access, and you will get a warning if all the extension accessed websites can be accessed for free.

Inbuilt translation

Safari also has an inbuilt translator that translates seven languages with one click, so you can read the entire website in another language without installing an extension.

Inbuilt Translated includes English, Spanish, Chinese, French, German, Russian, and Brazilian Portuguese.

Password management

For passwords stored on the iCloud Keychain, Safari now makes sure that it has not been compromised in any data breaches known. If the password is compromised, Safari warns you that you can change it.

YouTube and Netflix in 4K

macOS Big Sur supports Safari's 4K HDR YouTube video, allowing you to watch full-resolution movies in full resolution rather than 1080p. It also supports 4K HDR and Dolby Vision content from Netflix, but Mac owners need a Mac 2018 or later with a T2 chip that can watch 4K Netflix content on Safari while Big Sur is running.

Messages

Messages is now a Mac Catalyst app and is more compatible with Messaging application on iOS devices with similar capabilities, including some new features introduced in iOS 14.

Up to nine of your important conversations can be placed at the top of the Messaging application, at the top of the app, displayed as circular images. When someone types, a typing indicator notifies you and a new message and Tapbacks animates through the pin.

Group Chat can be personalized with pictures, Memoji, or emoji, and Mentions allows you to direct messages to a specific person. If the active group discussion is silent and someone in the conversation @mentions you, you can have it send a message so that you don't forget the most important moment of the conversation.

The messaging app includes a Memoji sticker (which can be pre-created on a Mac with a Memoji editor).

The search in the message is organized and the search results in pictures, phrases, and organize links.

Maps

According to reports, Apple has improved the Maps for Mac, introduced a number of features that were previously limited to iOS.

Bike routes can be configured on a Mac and routes to the account level, multiple paths, steps, and more, including electric vehicle power plants can be configured on a Mac along with additional options and sent to iOS.

Guides created by trusted brands and partners list suggestions for restaurants, shops, and tours in different cities around the world and you can create your own guides and share them with loved ones.

macOS Big Sur features look around in the Maps, so you can see the cities in detail, on the street level, and on the indoor view.

You can watch live updates of the shared ETAs in the Maps app, so you can track the progress of the person who actually shared the ETA on your Mac.

Spotlight

Searching using the Spotlight feature in the browser is displayed in a more precise list that makes it faster and easier to read results.

Quick look in the Spotlight feature, allows you to preview any document or website with editing tools as quickly as possible. The Quick View tool can be used without editing software for faster editing.

Focus menu in Safari, Pages, Keynotes, and more are now powered by spotlight.

App Store

A **nutrition label** for applications on the App Store and the Mac App Store was added by Apple, where you will find information from the creator about what information is being collected and if it will be used to track you across other apps and pages, in order for you to be able to make informed decisions about the applications you are downloading.

Apple Arcade incorporates a deeper Game Center integration, so you can find popular games with your friends, watch games with successes and sculptures, and see your gaming achievement with Game Center profile.

Photos

The Photo app has the latest enhancement tool to remove unnecessary items from pictures and has all the editing tools for image and video editing.

Vibrance can be applied to the image, the filter intensity and the result of the light can be adjusted to adjust the bottom.

AirPods

With macOS Big Sur and iOS 14, AirPods automatically switches between the same iCloud account and the same active devices.

So if you watch a video on your iPhone and then switch to Mac, AirPods can switch between iPhone and Mac without using Bluetooth controls to change your devices.

Apple Music

Apple Music's **For You** interface, which features artist interviews and a specific playlist for one place, has been replaced by **Listen Now**. It is just like **for you**, but more attention is paid to personal content and new releases.

The Apple Music search has a variety of categories and music based on categories such as Summer Sounds to make it easier to find something new to listen to.

Notes

As with iOS, the Pinned Notes section can be expanded or dropped, with new writing methods and configuration options, and can be accessed quickly with the new Quick Style feature.

The search includes **Top Hits** with the most important suggestions, and the scanning features of the continuity camera are even better, resulting in significant changes as the auto-cropping improves.

Weather

The weather widget features government notifications of adverse weather events, gives details of drastic changes in the weather, and gives details of the next hour's precipitation.

HOW TO SETUP YOUR DEVICE

If you are new to Mac and want to set up your MacBook, you may want to get ready before you get started. If you follow the on-screen instructions, it will be easy to set up your new Mac.

- Press the Power button on your Mac to switch it on.
- Choose a language.
  This is the language that your computer will write on the system.
- Click the Continue button.

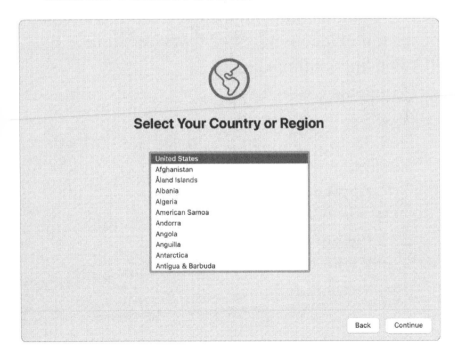

- Select the location of the keyboard.
  Whatever the keyboard looks physically, this is how what you type will be keyed on your computer.
- Click the Continue button.
- Select your Wi-Fi network.
  If you are connecting to the Internet via Ethernet, select another network option, and select Ethernet.
- If you use Wi-Fi, enter your Wi-Fi password.
- Click the Continue button.
  This can take a few minutes. You can see the wheels spin this is normal.
- If you are setting up your Mac as a new computer, choose **do not transfer data now**.
- Click the Continue button.
- Check this box to **enable location services on this Mac**.
  This service is essentially used for Siri, Maps, Spotlight services, and many more. If you do not want Apple to access your location, please do not check this box.
- Click the Continue button.
- Sign in with your Apple ID.
  Use the same Apple ID you use on your iPhone, iPad, Apple TV, and other iCloud services on

other Macs to configure the service on your device.

If you do not have an Apple ID, you can then create one on your Mac or register on your iPhone or iPad.

- Click the Continue button.
- Then there is a window allowing you to enable Siri, which will allow the active assistant to perform various tasks on the Mac.

- The next step is to set up iCloud (if you already signed in with your Apple ID). iCloud synchronizes up your contacts, calendars, your email account, web browsing data, reminders, and notes.
- You can choose whether your interface is dark or light, or auto. Which you can choose here - but you can easily change the situation later by opening system preferences, then click on general after that pick any appearance option
- Set up Touch ID
- Set up apple pay

20

HOW TO TRANSFER DATA FROM AN OLD MAC TO A NEW ONE

The Migration Assistant makes it easy to transfer data from your old Mac directly or from a Time Machine backup. You can also connect two Macs over Wi-Fi, Thunderbolt, FireWire, or Ethernet. Copying old data to your new computer will allow you to work on your new Mac at no cost.

Before you begin

Update your software - you need to update your software first.

Label your old Mac - If you have not already done so, make sure you name the old Mac. Open System preference> Sharing> and enter a name in the computer field.

Connect your old and new computers to a power source - both devices must be connected to a power source so that battery does not run out in the middle of the migration process.

Using immigrant helpers

Step 1: On a new Mac:

- Click on **go** on the toolbar of your Mac.
- Select the Utilities folder.
- Launch **migrant Assistant**

- Choose how you want to transfer data, either from a Mac, backup Time Machine, or startup disk.
- Click the Continue button.

Step 2: On the old Mac of yours:

- On the toolbar of your old Mac click on **GO**.
- Select the Utilities folder.
- Launch migrant Assistant

- Select the option to use the Migration Assistant on your Mac. Then click the "Continue" button.

Step 3: On a new Mac:

- When requested to choose a time machine backup, Mac or any other startup disk simply pick the **other mac** option.
- Click the Continue button.

Step 4: On the old Mac of yours:

- Confirm that the security code displayed on the old Mac is the same as the code on the new Mac.
- Click the Continue button.

Step 5: On the new Mac:

- Select the data to send.
- Click the Continue button.

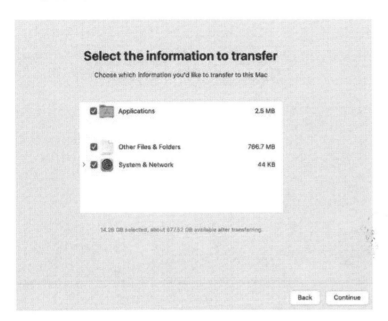

When the migration assistant is done, log in to your account that was moved to the new Mac to view its files.

FEATURES OF THE M1 MACBOOK AIR

In November, Apple released its first MacBook Air, with the Arm-based M1 chip. The M1 chip received good reviews for its performance and efficiency.

This chapter would work you through what you need to know about it.

Design

The M1 MacBook Air has no external changes compared to previous models. It continues to be made of aluminum alloy and is available in Silver, Space Gray, and Gold.

The MacBook Air has a thick to thin design in front of the device. The MacBook Air is 0.63 inches thick at its thick point and 0.16 inches thinner at its thinnest point Slightly thicker than the 2019 MacBook Pro.

In terms of size, the MacBook Air is 11.97 inches long, 8.36 inches wide, weighs 2.8 pounds, and is 0.2 pounds shorter than the 13-inch MacBook Pro.

Display

Since 2018, the MacBook Air has been using Retina displays that are lighter, sharper, and clearer than non-Retina displays. The MacBook Air features a resolution of about 2560 x 1,600 inches with 227 pixels per inch and a total of 4 million pixels, with a total brightness of 400 nit.

The display on the MacBook Air supports True Tone, which is designed to change the color of the screen to match room lighting. True Tone works with many light-emitting diodes integrated into the MacBook Air, which can measure room brightness and color temperature.

After finding a white balance, the MacBook Air can adjust the color and intensity of the screen to room lighting for a more natural and paper-like viewing experience that cuts down the straining of the eyes.

It now supports P3 wide colors that bring clearer and more realistic colors and improved sRGB colors over the previous models. Wide color gives 25 percent more color than sRGB.

Keyboard

The M1 MacBook Air makes use of the Magic Keyboard.

The scissor mechanism on the MacBook Air keyboard provides 1mm of stable key and key travel feel, it also uses an apple design rubber dome that saves a lot of potential energy to give out a more responsive key press.

Launchpad and keyboard control of brightness are replaced by Spotlight search, DND, and dictation, and there is an emoji Fn key.

The keyboard also has a backlight key, which is controlled by an ambient light sensor to illuminate the buttons in the dark room.

Touch ID

The M1 MacBook Air has a fingerprint Touch ID sensor near the function button above the keyboard.

Touch ID is been powered by Secure Enclave, which stores your fingerprint and personal information.

The sensor ID on the MacBook can be used to unlock the Mac when the finger is placed on the sensor instead of the password. It replaces password as well for password-protected apps and can be used to make purchases in Apple Pay in Safari.

Trackpad

The MacBook Air has a large Force Touch trackpad that has no traditional buttons and is used by the Force Sensor, allowing users to click anywhere on the trackpad to achieve the same results.

Port

Thunderbolt 3 / USB-4 USB-C ports are included in the MacBook Air. The Thunderbolt 3 and MacBook Air can support 4K, 5K, and 6K displays and can be integrated into the eGPU for faster image capabilities if needed.

The 6K display allows the MacBook Air M1 to work with the XDR Pro Display and other 6K displays. The MacBook Air supports single 6K monitor, a single 5K monitor, or two 4K monitors.

With two Thunderbolt 3 ports, the device has a 3.5mm headphone jack on the other side.

M1 Apple Silicone Chip

The MacBook Air was one of the first Macs to be updated with a chip designed for Apple-based Arm, not an Intel chip like previous MacBook Air models but rather the M1 chip.

M1 is Apple's first chip system created for Mac, which includes a processor, GPU, I/O, security features, and RAM. Apple says it will allow for longer battery life and better performance.

Like Apple's latest A14 chips, the M1 is based on a 5-nano process, which makes it smaller and more efficient than previous Apple chips. There are 16 billion transistors, and Apple says it has the most on one chip.

Speed improvement

The M1 has an 8-core CPU and an 8-core GPU. The CPU has four impact cores and four high-performance cores. When you do simple things like surfing the web or reading e-mails, the MacBook Air includes advanced features to save battery life, but high-performance kernels are used for more intensive tasks such as image and video editing.

GPU

The M1 chip includes an 8-core GPU (which means it's not a standalone chip), and Apple calls them the fastest integrated graphics in the world on personal computers. It can take 25,000 threads at a time and combine graphics efficiency with low energy consumption.

Neutral engine

The MacBook Air has a new and more advanced Neural engine that is 9x faster for machine learning issues. The engine has a 16-core design that can run 11 trillion operation per second.

No fans

The MacBook Air has no fans for cooling purposes. Instead, the aluminum heat spreader separates the heat and allows it to work quietly.

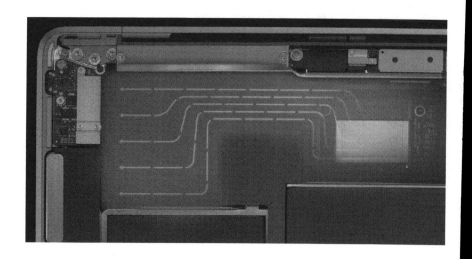

Battery life

The M1 MacBook Air has an impressive battery life that is higher than the battery life of previous-generation models.

The 49.9WHr battery, similar to previous-generation models, lasts up to 15 hours when you access the Internet and up to 18 hours when you watch a movie through Apple TV.

Connectivity

The MacBook Air supports 802.11ax WiFi, also known as Wi-Fi 6, and the new 802.11ac WiFi protocol is faster and more efficient than the old WiFi. It is also compatible with Bluetooth 5 as well.

Speakers and microphones

It features a three-array microphone with built-in speakers for various stereo speakers to watch, Apple TV, or play iOS games and FaceTime calls.

FaceTime camera

A 720p HD camera is built-in the MacBook Air for FaceTime call. Apple has been using 720p face cameras for a number of years now and has not improved the quality, but this year the M1 chip allows for clearer and sharper images.

The M1 chip provides better sound reduction for more detailed information in shadows and key moments, and uses Neural Motion, Natural Balance, and Face Detection to adjust color reduction

Storage space

The MacBook Air maintains a solid-state of storage up to 2TB. At the bottom of the MacBook Air, the storage starts at 256 GB and the MacBook Air's SSD reaches 2x faster than the previous generation SSD's.

SSD performance confirms that the MacBook Air's SSD is significantly faster, with a writing speed of 2190MB / s and a read speed of 2676MB / s. This is twice as fast as the SSD on the previous MacBook Air.

BASIC SETTINGS

Knowing your way around

Desktop, menus bar, and Mac help

The first thing you see on your MacBook Air is the desktop to quickly open apps, search for anything on your MacBook Air and web, organize your files, and much more.

Help menu. The Help menu for your device is available always in the menu bar. To get help, click the Help menu and select macOS Help to open the macOS User Guide.

Airdrop

AirDrop helps you to easily shares files on Mac, iPhone, iPad, and iPod touch nearby. Devices do not need to share the same Apple ID.

Send a file from Finder. Control-tap the one you want to send, select Share> AirDrop, and then select the device you want to send it to. Otherwise, click the Finder icon in the Dock, then click AirDrop in the left pane (or select Go> AirDrop). When the person you want to send the file to appears in the window, drag the file from the desktop or another Finder window to them. When you send a file to someone, the recipient can choose to accept the file or not.

Send a file to an application. When using an application like Page or Preview, click the Share button⌥ and select AirDrop, then select the device you want to send the item to.

Control who can send items to you via AirDrop. Click the Control Center icon⬛ on the menu bar, click the AirDrop icon ◉, and then select "Contacts Only" or "All". You can also turn on AirDrop or turn it off.

Making use of AirPlay on a Mac

Use the Airplay screen mirror to display what's on your MacBook Air on the big screen. Connect your Apple TV to HDTV and ensure the Apple TV is on the one wifi network with your MacBook air, so that you can mirror your MacBook Air to your TV screen or use your HDTV as a second display. You can also play movies directly on your HDTV without showing it on your desktop - more convenient when you want to play movies, but also want your work to be private.

Use screen mirroring to mirror your desktop. Click the Center Control icon ⚏ in the menu bar, click the Screen Mirror screen icon ▢, and then select Apple TV. When AirPlay is functioning, the icon is blue.

Play a web video that does not show your desktop. When you see a web video with an AirPlay logo , click on the icon, then select Apple TV.

Note: If the image does not match your HDTV screen after mirroring, adjust the screen size to the best picture size by clicking the AirPlay icon in the video, and then pick any option underneath the **match desktop sizes to** section.

How to extend battery life

You can do this by reducing screen brightness, closing the application, and disconnecting peripheral devices that you are not making use of. Tap on battery in the system preferences to change your power settings. If your MacBook Air is In sleep mode while you connect a device to it, the device's battery may be drained.

How to check your battery usage history

Click Battery in System Preference, then click Usage History to see how your battery has been used in the last 24 hours or 10 days.

Works with wireless devices

The MacBook Air uses Bluetooth technology to connect Bluetooth keyboards, mouse, trackpads, headphones, and more can connect wirelessly to the device.

Connect the Bluetooth device. Turn the device on so that it can be discovered, then open System Preferences and tap Bluetooth. Select the device from the list, and click the Connect button. The device stays connected until you remove it. Control - tap on the device name to remove it.

Turn Bluetooth on or off. Click the Control Center icon on the menu bar, click the Bluetooth icon, and then click the Control to activate or deactivate Bluetooth.

If you do not see the Bluetooth icon in the menu bar, you can add it. Click the Bluetooth icon in the control center, click the Bluetooth option, and then select **Show Bluetooth in the menu bar**.

Get the best of Apple Music.

In the music app, click on browse on the sidebar to view new music and special releases from Apple Music, a paid music streaming service. Download and stream over 50 million songs without ads.

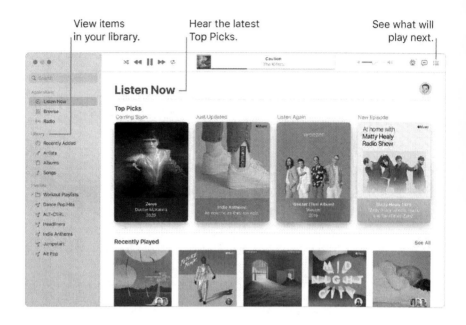

Viewing the lyrics of a song

If you are playing a song and want to sing along but you do not know the lyrics, you can simply tap on the lyrics icon 💬 at the top right corner of your screen to show a panel with the lyrics for the present song (if any).

Using apple news

Apple News is the only store for news and information provided by the editor and dedicated to you. You can even save articles for future reading either offline or on other devices. Apple News + lets you read hundreds of magazines, popular magazines, and premium digital publishers for a one-time monthly price.

To follow your favorite channels and topics of interest and see them in the today's feed and sidebar. Enter a source or topic in the search field, and click the Add button ✝ to follow it.

If you are reading a text and want to save it for later, simply pick File> save story. To view the article some other time, click on the saved story close to the top of the sidebar. When you sign in with the same Apple ID on any of your other devices you would be able to access articles on the devices.

Maximizing the use of Notes

Notes have more use than just text. Write down a quick thought or add a checklist, website links, etc. Shared folder allows all file folders to be shared with a group, and anyone can participate.

Tell Siri. State something like, **create a new comment**.

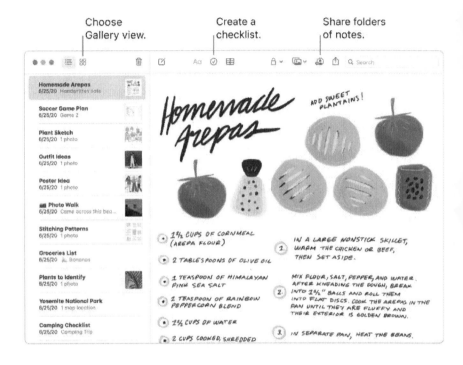

Choose Gallery view.

Create a checklist.

Share folders of notes.

When you log in with your Apple ID and iCloud is turn on for Notes, it will be updated on all your devices, so you can create a to-do list on your Mac, then check things on the iPhone.

You can customize your toolbar by Right-clicking anywhere in the bar to open a customized window. Simply drag the items you want into the toolbar.

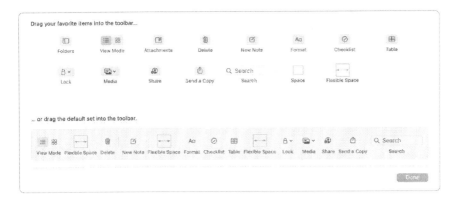

To add a table, simply click the table button 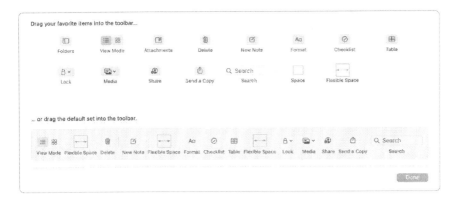 to add a table to your notes. You can also copy and paste a table from websites or other applications.

You can set a password to lock notes that you do not want others to see. To set a password, select Notes> preference, and click the set password option. To lock a note, select the note and select File> Lock note.

Upload files, site previews, map locations, and more to notes

• In the Notes app on your Mac, click the note in the note list, or double-click it in the gallery view.

47

If you choose a note that is locked you will not be able to add video, audio, PDF, or files.

- To add any attachment, do any of the below:
  - ❖ From the desktop: drag the file into the note.
  - ❖ From the Photo Library: drag the photo directly from the Photo Library in to the note.
  - ❖ From other apps, such as Maps, Safari, Photos, and more: in the app click the Share button 📤, then select Notes.

    The share button is not available in all applications.

    You can also select a few text or images by control-tapping your selection and then select Share> Notes.

To resize an image, scanned doc, or PDF file in the note, control-tap the attachment, and then select the view as large image or view as small image option.

Maximizing the use of Podcasts

Use Apple Podcast to watch, subscribe, and listen to your favorite podcasts on your Mac.

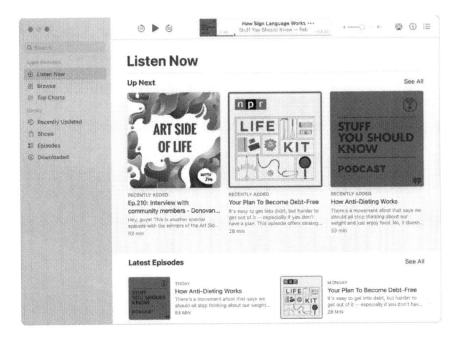

Click the Add button ✛ to save a single episode to your library. Click Subscribe to follow the new episodes for the entire podcast. Click the Download button ☁ to download the podcast for offline listening.

You can use AirPlay to play podcasts, music, or radio with an external speaker. Tap on the Control Center logo that is in the menu bar, tap on Screen Mirror after that choose a speaker that is available.

Maximizing the stocks application

The stock application is the best way to keep track of the market on your Mac. Check for prices on your custom watchlist, click on a stock to find out more details and an exchange chart, and read what is driving the market, with news from apple.

Click to read the latest business news.

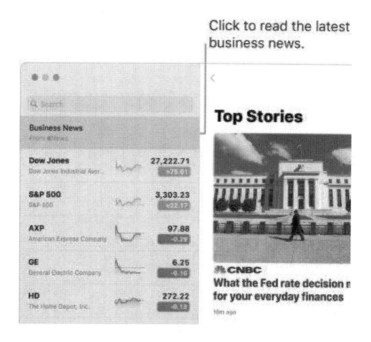

To add a stock to your watchlist, enter the company name or stock logo in the Search box, control-tap the stock in the search results, and tap on add to watch list. To delete a stock, control-tap on the icon of the stock and click the Remove from watchlist button. You can also control-tap a stock to open it in a new window or tab.

When checking out your watch list, click the green or red button at the bottom of each price to toggle between price fluctuations, interest rate changes, and market capitalization. The watch list also includes color-coded lines that monitor day-to-day performance.

How to make use of voice memos

Voice memos make it easy to capture personal reminders, lectures from class, or even conversations or ideas about a song. With iCloud, you can access voice memos that were recorded on your iPhone in your MacBook Air.

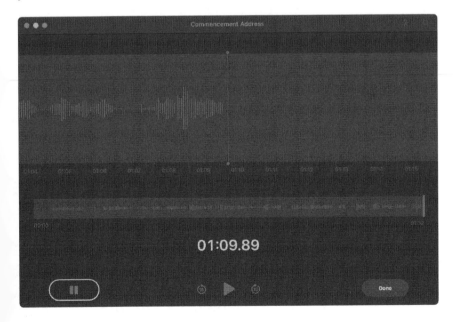

Press the recording button ● to start recording, after you have finished recording click on **done**. You can change the name of the recording to make it easier to know them. Click on the default name, then enter a new name. Click the play button ▶. to play your recording.

Your voice memo is available on all your devices when you sign in with the same Apple ID. You can access what you recorded on your iPhone or iPad via Mac.

To create a folder to keep your voice memos organized. Click the sidebar button ▭. to add a folder, and then click the New Folder button at the bottom end of your sidebar. Enter a folder name, then click the Save button. To add a recording to the folder, click and hold the Option button while dragging the recording to the folder.

You can improve the voice memos sound quality by reducing background noise and room clutter. Click Edit at the top of the voice memos window, click the Play button, and click the Enhance button ✷.

Mark recordings as Favorites.

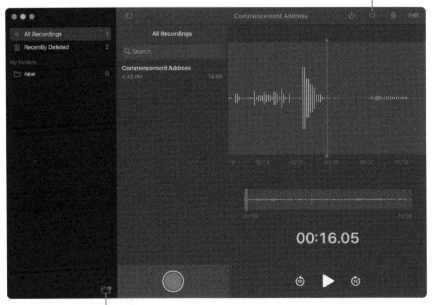

Create new folders to
organize your recordings.

53

SIRI

macOS Big Sur and Siri on Mac go deeper into the software than the iPhone and iPad. You can search for files, verify your situation, and understand the contextual language, so you can ask questions and follow up with related questions.

Activating Siri on Mac

- If you want to enable Siri on your Mac, click the Apple logo at the top left part of the screen, then select System Preferences.

 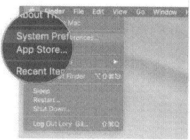

- Select Siri.
- Check the box on the left side of the window to activate talk to Siri.

- Pick a language and then select the voice Siri would use.

 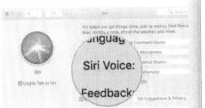

- If you do not want Sori to speak, turn off Voice feedback.
- Select Mic input from internal or external accessory.

 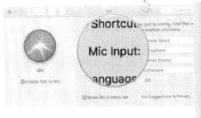

How to activate Type to Siri

You can write your question to Siri without asking it loudly.

- Tap on the Apple logo, after that click on Systems Preference

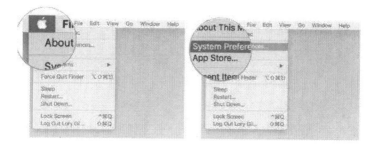

- Click on accessibility, then click Siri, after that check the box for **enable type to Siri**.

Once you have activated **type to Siri**, a text field appears above the keyboard when you launch the virtual private assistant. Just write your question and Siri will answer it as best as it can.

Don't forget that Siri will speak out to you, so if you don't want to hear and scare people around you, lower your Mac or turn off Siri's voice feedback

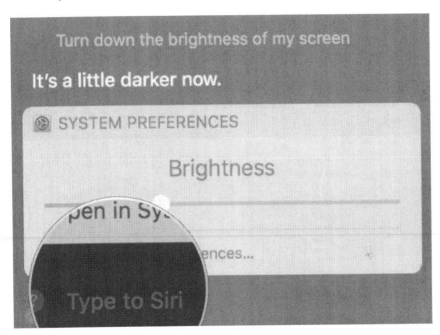

How to use keyboard shortcuts to activate Siri

You can tap on Siri on your Dock or the Menu button at the top of the screen. But if you like keyboard shortcuts, it is also possible.

- Tap on the Apple logo, then Select **systems preference**
- Select Siri.
- Pick a keyboard shortcut under keyboard shortcut. As a rule, you hold **Command-Space**, but you can choose from **hold Option-Space**, **Function-Space**, or personalize it to any combination you need.

Once the keyboard shortcut is set, you can hold both keys you assign until Siri appears.

How to use Siri on a Mac with AirPods or Beats headphones

If you have Beats headphones or AirPods that support Siri when voice-activated (Powerbeats Pro only now), you can ask Siri for help.

- Tap on the Apple logo of the top left part of your screen, after that select Systems Preference.
- Select Siri.
- Check the box to **listen for Hey Siri on the headphones**.
- If you want to activate Siri when the Mac is locked with tour voice, check the box for **Allow Siri when locked**.

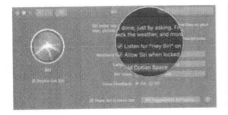 

How to pin Siri response to notification center

You can pin all Siri search results in the notification center. This can be very helpful if you want to keep track of documents maybe for work purposes.

- Click the Siri icon in the menu bar or Dock, or use the keyboard shortcuts to activate Siri.
- Tell Siri to search for files, docs, or carry out a web search.
- When the search results appear in the Siri window, click the Plus (+) button next to the search results.

The search results that Siri provides would be attached to your notification centre. To delete it, go to the Search segment of your notification Center and click the X.

SAFARI

Safari is Apple's website browser. Go to websites, bookmark your favorite pages, and more. Here's what you need to know to get started with Safari on macOS Big Sur.

How to bookmark a website

If you really like what you read online or want to get to your favorite pages quickly, you can bookmark it easily!

- Launch Safari from Dock or Finder on your Mac.
- Go to the **web page** you plan to bookmark.
- Press **Command-D** on the keyboard.
- Give your bookmark a name.
- Press the Add or tap the **Return** button on the keyboard.
- Select View in the menu bar on the top left side of the screen.
- Select your **show favorite Bar**.

Now the bookmarked pages you add to Favorites will appear at the bottom of the address bar, so you can click on them easily. In addition, every time you click on an address, your favorite will show up as suggested sites.

You can also view your bookmarks by clicking on the **show side bar button** beside the address bar, after that click on the **bookmark tab**, which looks like a book

How to add a webpage to your reading list

Adding a page to your reading list allows you to save this page and then read it some other time. The best part is that you can go through your reading list without an internet connection.

- Go to the page you want to add to your reading list.

- Press **shift-command-D** on the keyboard, or select a **bookmark** from the menu bar, and then tap on **add to Reading List**.

To view your reading list, tap on the **show sidebar button** beside the address bar, and then tap on the reading list tab. It resembles a pair of glasses, after that pick the item you want. To remove an item from the reading list simply control-click the item, tap on the **remove item**

Enabling private browsing

Allows you to browse the Internet without saving your personal search, the pages you visit, your search history, or your AutoFill profile.

- Click the file in the menu bar at the top right of the screen.
- Click the New Private Window. You can simply press **shift-command-N** on the keyboard.

How to view a website's privacy reports

You can view security reports every time you visit a page, starting with the macOS Big Sur. To do this:

- Go to the webpage you are looking for.
- Click the Privacy Report button on the left side of the address bar.
- To view the report in full, select the data icon.

- Review the report, which includes a list of tackers who have been prevented by Safari from running on the site.
- Click the **red circle** at the left to go away from the report.

How to add an extension to Safari

Browser extensions are plugins that add new functionality to Safari. They can block ads and more. There are many free extensions that provide you with updates, security, entertainment, and more!

Note: Although extensions are free, the services or applications that they are provided from may not.

- Click Safari on the menu bar at the top left of the screen.
- Click on **Safari Extensions**.

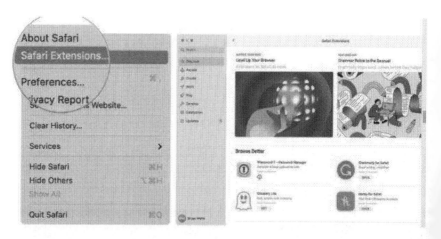

You will be taken to the mac App Store safari extension page, where you can download extensions. Once the installation is complete, open the application to install in the Safari toolbar.

66

How to share a website

If you come across a page you want your friends or family to see, you can share it in many ways.

- Go to the page you want to share.
- Click on the sharing sheet button on the right side of the safari window.
- Select a sharing method. You can share with email, messages, AirDrop, notes, reminders, and third-party applications.

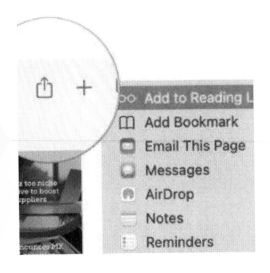

How to use the reader's view

- Go to the websites.

- Click the Reader View button. It is the lines on the left side of the address bar.

To change the background colour simply click on the As on the right side of your address bar, then click on a background color you like, you can also click any font you would want to make use of.

You can also make the fonts bigger or smaller by clicking on the **A** the big A makes it bigger while the small A make the fonts smaller

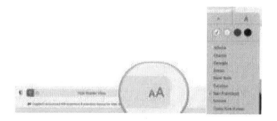

Personalize the toolbar

A functional toolbar with the keys used regularly is necessary to use Safari. For example, if you do not use the Home button, you can remove it. If you need a button for sidebar, you can add it.

To make changes, right-click on the toolbar and select **customize the Toolbar**. Then drag the button you need from the window that popup into the toolbar or the ones you do not want from the toolbar to the window. You can also customize the buttons as you wish. Tap on the **Done** button when you are through.

Turn off popups from notifications

If you visit many blogs or news sites, you can find ads to subscribe to new posts. Instead of rejecting

the request each time, you can completely disable
this feature.

Click **Safari> preferences** on the menu bar and
select the **website** tab. Click the notification on the
left. Then untick the **Allow website to request
permission to send notifications** option on the
bottom of the page.

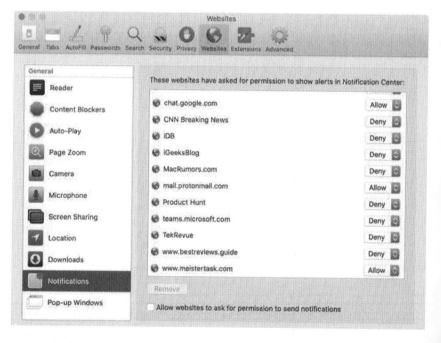

You can also click on the drop-down box on the
right side of any page in the list to allow or deny
notifications for specific sites.

Save the pages in PDF format

Exporting websites to PDF does not require special extensions when using Safari. Go to the page and click **File> Export in PDF format**.

Then, select where to save the page and export it.

Use auto-fill

You can speed up the login process with AutoFill for frequently visited pages that require a username and password. The AutoFill feature works with your details from Contacts application, the credit card you choose to store, and other information.

To activate AutoFill, click **Safari> preferences** on your menu bar. Select the tab for AutoFill and tick the boxes for what you want to include. You can edit the information with the appropriate button.

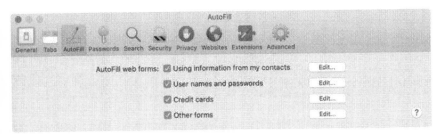

TOUCH ID

For years now, both the MacBook Pro and MacBook Air models have come with a Touch ID built into the keyboard. If you are new to Mac, setting up a Touch ID takes a while, but it will make a big difference in your daily life.

How does Touch ID work?

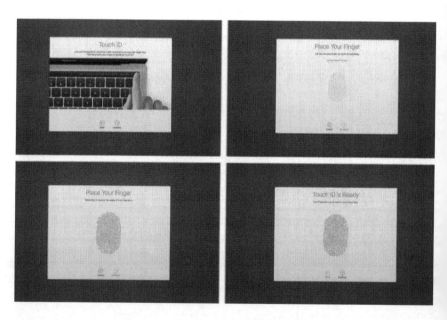

The Touch ID on the MacBook is the name of Apple's fingerprint sensor. This is a form of biometric security that is easier to enter than a passcode or password, especially on iPhones and iPads that use it dozens of times a day.

How to add a fingerprint

- Tap on the Apple menu logo after that select systems preference.
- Select the Touch ID preference bar.

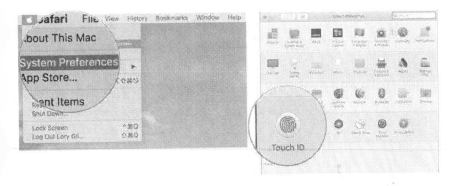

- Tap on Add a fingerprint.
- Enter your password.

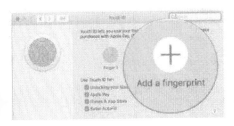

Adhere to the guidelines and keep your fingers in the Touch ID sensor until the registration is complete.

How to name a fingerprint

- Tap on the Apple menu icon on the top right corner of your screen after that choose systems preference.
- Select the Touch ID selection bar.

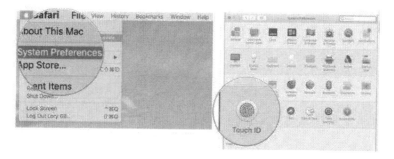

- Press the Tab key to go through the registered fingerprint
- Change your footprint name.
- Press the return button.

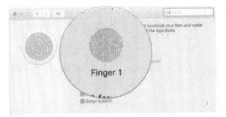 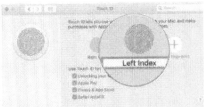

How to delete fingerprints

- Tap on the Apple menu icon on the top right corner of your screen after that choose systems preference.
- Select the Touch ID selection bar.

- Move around the fingerprint you want to delete until you see X in the upper left corner then tap on it.
- Enter your password
- Click Delete to delete.

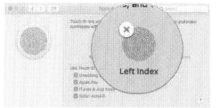 

How to change your Touch ID settings

You can choose which fingerprint you want to use. As a rule, all three options have been ticked, but you can change them by unticking the box beside them.

- Go to the Apple menu
- Select system preferences.
- Select the Touch ID selection bar.

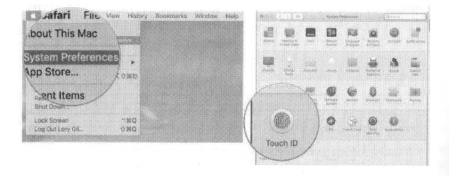

- Tick or untick any options you want

The "Use Touch ID" option includes:

- AutoFill Safari
- iTunes and the app store
- Apple Pay
- Unlocking your Mac

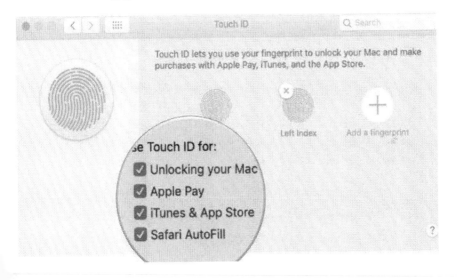

APPLE PAY

The iPhone, Apple Watch, and Mac all support Apple Pay, below are steps to set up Apple Pay and manage your wallet.

Setting up Apple Pay

You need to set up Apple Pay before you can use it on your Mac.

- Open Safari on Mac.
- Tap on Safari in the top left part of your Mac.
- Click system preference.

 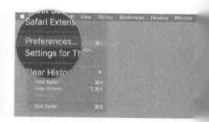

- Click the **Privacy** tab.
- Check the box next to **Apple Pay and Apple Card** to allow the site to be interested in payment options.

How to setup apple pay on your touch bar mac

If you have a MacBook Air or MacBook Pro with a Touch ID, you can allow payments from the keyboard. But before you can do that, you need to add your credit card to Apple Pay. You need to do this when you first set up your Mac, but you can setup Apple Pay through the System Prefers software whenever you want.

- Open the system preferences.
- Tap the Wallet and Apple Pay icon.

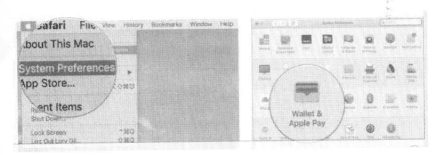

- Click the Add Card button to add a new credit or debit card.

- Place your card in front of your iSight camera to automatically read your number or enter your card information manually.

- Click the **Next** button to verify your credit card number.
- Check the card expiration date and enter the three-digit security code.
- Click the **Next** button.

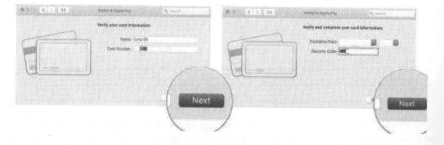

- Press the accept button to accept the term and condition of your card.
- Select a verification method to verify your card.
- Click the **Next** button.

- Enter the verification code sent to you with your chosen method.
- Click the **Next** button.

How to manage your Apple Pay card on a Mac

You can see more details from the System Prefers Wallet & Apple Pay area after installing a card on a Mac that supports Touch ID.

- Open System Preferences on Mac.
- Tap the Wallet and Apple Pay icon.
- To see your credit card information—which includes your account number, billing address, bank contact info, -Select it from the side bar.

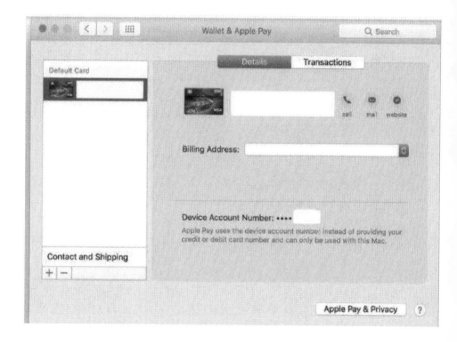

Changing your default card

If you have added more than one card, you can change it.

- Open System Preferences on Mac
- Tap the Wallet and Apple Pay icon.
- In the drop-down menu at the bottom of the screen, select the card you want to make your default card.

How to remove a card

- Open System Preferences on Mac
- Tap the Wallet and Apple Pay icon.
- Select the card you want to delete on the border.
- Click the - (delete) button at the bottom of the sidebar.

How to manage your shipping and contact information

You can view and edit your current profile (email, shipping address, and phone number) on the setting screen.

- Open System Preferences on Mac.
- Tap the Wallet and Apple Pay icon.
- Select the Contact and Delivery options at the bottom of the sidebar.

To change your shipping address, e-mail address, or phone number, select the option you want to edit from the drop-down menu. It also allows you to add new addresses, e-mail, or phone numbers.

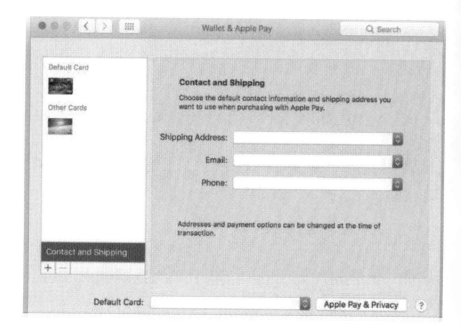

How to manage your billing address

If you want to change your billing address, you can select the card you want.

- Open System Preferences on Mac
- Tap the Wallet and Apple Pay icon.
- Select the card you want to change in the side bar.
- Choose **add a new billing address** under the dropdown of **billing address**.
- Enter the **new billing address** and click **Save**.

84

85

FACETIME

Although messages is a good way to send an instant message, you may want to talk to people at times. This is where FaceTime comes in. FaceTime connectivity allows people to make video and voice calls when you need a private message.

Follow this chapter to learn how to make FaceTime for Mac.

How to set up FaceTime on Mac

Getting started with FaceTime is very simple and all you need is an Apple ID.

- Open FaceTime on Mac.

- Enter your Apple ID email address and password and click Sign In.

How to make a FaceTime call

- Open FaceTime on Mac.
- If you are making a new call, click on the search bar.
- Enter the name, number, or email address you want to contact.
- Tap on Video or audio.
- If you picked audio, click on **FaceTime Audio** or your contact phone number.

Adding an email address to FaceTime

If you have multiple email addresses or usernames, you can create a FaceTime account so you can be accessed with all of these addresses. But you don't put this on FaceTime. Instead, you need to go to System Preferences.

- Open the system options from the Dock or Applications folder.
- Click on Apple ID.

- Click on name, phone, email.
- Click the + button under the Reachable segment.

- Type in the email address you plan to make use of.
- Click the **Next** button.
- If requested, enter the verification code sent to this email address. Your code will be verified automatically.

How to set up FaceTime calls ringtone

Make your FaceTime experience worthwhile with a new ringtone.

- With FaceTime opens, tap on FaceTime on the navigation bar.
- Click preference.

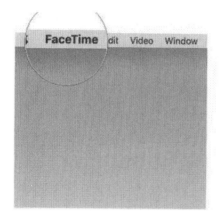
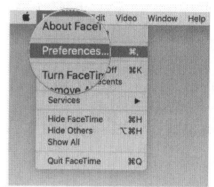

- Click the drop-down menu next to the ringtone.
- Choose your favorite ringtone.

How to set up location

- With FaceTime opens, click FaceTime on the navigation bar.
- Click preferences.
- Tap on the dropdown menu beside Location.
- Choose the location you like.

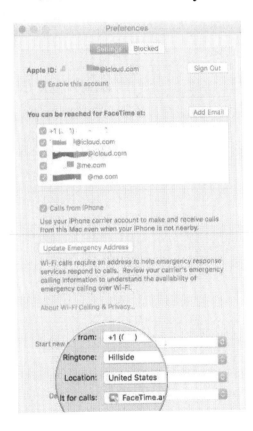

KEYBOARD

The keyboard shortcut of Apple mac allows you to be more efficient and effective.

One of the most important tools to monitor production in office work is the use of keyboard shortcuts. The right shortcut can turn the keyboard on the typewriter into a command center for your computer.

By clicking on a few combinations, you can often do whatever you normally do with your mouse, trackpad, or other input device, with just your keyboard.

To use the keyboard shortcut, click and hold one or more buttons, and then click the last shortcut key. For example, to use Command-C (copy) hold down the command key, then press the C key, then release the two buttons. Mac Menus and keyboards often use icons for certain keys, including modifiers:

Shift ⇧

Command (Cmd) ⌘

Control (or Ctrl) ^

Options (or Alt) ⌥

Caps Lock ⇧

Fn

Some Apple keyboards have icons and special functions for display brightness ☀, keyboard brightness ☼, Mission Control, and much more. If these features are not available on the keyboard, you can create your own keyboard shortcuts and translate some of them.

Copy, paste, cute, and some other common shortcuts

- Command-X: Cut the selected items and copy them to the clipboard.
- Command-C: Copy the highlighted item to the clipboard.
- Command-V: Paste the contents of the board into the current doc or application.

93

- Command-Z: Undo the last command. You can also press Shift-Command-Z to reverse the undo command/ redo it.
- Command-A: Select all of the items.
- Command-F: Find something in the doc or open the search window.
- Command-G: Search again: Look for the next occurrence.
- Command-H: hide the front application window. Press Option-Command-H to see the front application but hide all the other applications.
- Command-P: Print the present doc
- Command-S: Save the current file.
- Command-T: Opens a new tab.
- Command-W: Close the window on the front. Press Option-Command-W to close all windows of the application.
- Option-Command-Esc: force quit an application.
- Control-Command-F: If it is supported by the application, make use of the application in full screen.
- Spacebar: Use Quick View to preview selected items.
- Command-tab: Go to the last used app in all open applications.

- Shift-Command-5: Take a screenshot or make a screen record. Use Shift-Command-3 or Shift-Command-4 for screenshots.
- Shift-Command-N: Creates a new folder in Finder.

System and finder shortcut

- Command-D: Duplicate the files you selected.
- Command-E: Remove the selected disk or volume.
- Command-F: Start the search on the spotlight in the Finder window.
- Shift-Command-C: Open the computer window.
- Shift-Command-D: launch the desktop folder.
- Shift-Command-F: Open the Recents window and show all the files you have recently viewed or modified.
- Shift-Command-H: Open the Home folder of your current macOS user account.
- Shift-Command-I: Open iCloud Drive.
- Shift-Command-K: launch the window of Network.
- Option-Command-L: launch the download folder.

- Shift-Command-N: Creates a new folder.
- Shift-Command-O: Launch the Docs folder.
- Shift-Command-P: Display or hide the Preview pane of the Finder window.
- Shift-Command-R: Open the AirDrop window.
- Shift-Command-T: hide or display the tab bar that is in the finder window.
- Control-Shift-Command-T: Adds Finder items selected into the dock
- Shift-Command-U: Open the Utilities folder.
- Option-command-D: hide or display the dock.
- Option-command-S: Hide or show the sidebar in the finders window.
- Command - Slash (/): Hide the status bar or show it in the Finder window.
- Command-J: Show your view options.
- Command-K: Open the Server Connection window.
- Command-N: Opens a New Finder window.
- Option-Command-N: Create a smart folder.
- Command-T: When a single tab in the Finder window opens, it shows or hides the tab bar.
- Option-Command-T: Show or hide the toolbar when a single tab opens in the Finder window.
- Option-Command-V: Move the clipboard files to the current location from their original location.

- Command-Y: Quickly preview selected files using quick look.
- Option-Command-Y: Browse the Quick View slideshow for selected files.
- Command - Bracket left ([): head over to the previous folder.
- Command - Bracket right (]): Go to the next folder.

Documents shortcuts

The format of these shortcuts may vary depending on the application you are making use of.

Command-I: put the selected text in italics, or undo it.

Command-K: Adds a web link.

Command-U: Line or remove selected text, or undo it.

Command-T: Show or hide the window for fonts.

Command-D: Select the Desktop folder from the Open dialog box or from the Save dialog box.

Shift-Command-Colon (:): Show the window for spelling and grammar.

Command-Semicolon (;): Find the misspelled words in the doc.

Fn - Top arrow: to scroll up by a page.

Fn - Down arrow: scroll down by a page

Fn - Left Arrow: Home: Slide to the beginning of the doc.

Fn - Right Arrow: End: Slide to the end of the doc.

Command - Up arrow: Move the point of insertion to the beginning of the doc.

Command - Down arrow: Move the point of insertion to the end of the doc.

Command - Left Arrow: Moves to the point of insertion to the starting of the present line.

Command - Right Arrow: move the point of insertion to the ending of the present line.

Options - Left arrow: Move the entry point to the beginning of the previous word.

Options - Right Arrow: Move the insertion point to the end of the next word.

Control-A: Slide to the beginning of a line or paragraph.

Control E: Jump to the end of a paragraph or line.

Control-F: move by a character forward.

Control-B: move by a character backward.

Shift - Command - Number (-): reduces the size of the selected item.

ICLOUD

With iCloud Drive, you can access all your files that store presently and are synced on the iCloud storage service of Apple. You can access iCloud Drive on your Mac on the Internet or in the Finder window. Here is the way.

Activating iCloud Drive

If you haven't activated iCloud Drive on your Mac yet, you can do it anytime.

- Click the Apple menu icon in the upper left corner of your Mac.
- Click systems preference.
- Click on the Apple ID.
- Check the box for iCloud Drive to activate it.

How to access iCloud Drive from the website

You can go to your iCloud file from the Internet on any device or computer.

- Go to iCloud.com on your browser.
- Enter the email address and password associated with the Apple ID.
- Click the arrow next to your password.

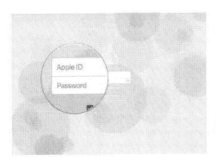
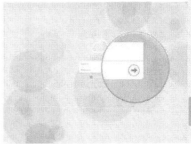

- If asked, enter the verification code sent to your trusted device to receive confirmations.
- Click on iCloud Drive.

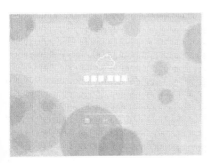

You can view or download files from the Web, transfer them to another folder, send to your email or delete as well.

How to access iCloud Drive from Finder on Mac

You can also access iCloud Drive on a Mac without using a browser in the Finder window.

- On your Mac, open the finder.
- Tap on iCloud Drive in the sidebar of the Finder.
- Double-click to open files.

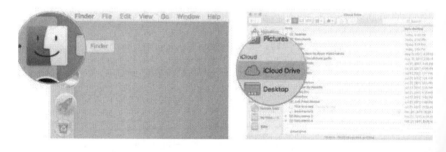

You can also search for iCloud Drive on Spotlight to quickly find iCloud Drive on your Mac.

How to deactivate iCloud Drive on Mac

If you don't want to keep iCloud Drive on your Mac, you can deactivate it.

- Click the Apple menu icon in the upper left corner of your Mac.
- Click systems preference.
- Click on the Apple ID.
- Uncheck the box beside iCloud Drive to deactivate it.

TIPS AND TRICKS

With macOS Big Sur, Apple has redesigned the entire macOS UI to be more like that of the iPhone and iPad. An iconic unMac-like dock might scare you at first, but many local apps with full desktops and open bars are undoubtedly examples of good design. In addition, macOS Big Sur comes with a number of interesting new features.

macOS Big Sur is a major update that brings new and exciting changes. Take advantage of your time to master the operating system as you see fit, change can be a bit difficult. You can also compile the following macOS Big Sur tips and tricks to learn how to better use the OS.

Now Playing menu item

There is a new menu bar for the media that is currently playing. It Looks like your widget that can be added in the notification center.

To activate the menu bar, go to System Preferences -> dock and menu bar, click the **now playing** button on the sidebar, and then tick the box next to **show in the menu bar.**

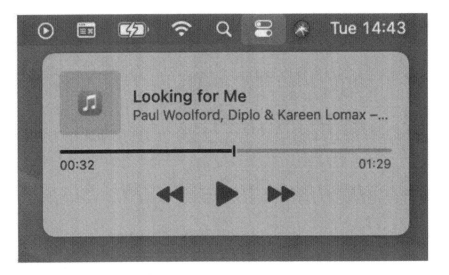

Play sound on startup options

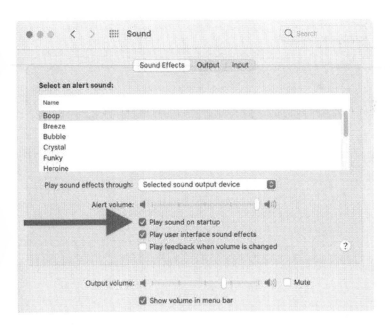

Now you can choose whether or not to play regular startup chime on your Mac without messing with Terminal commands. Go to System Preferences> Sound, and then tick the box next to the **play sound on startup**.

Personalize Safari start page

Safari on macOS 11 features a standalone start page that allows you to customize the different aspects of it.

While on the start page, click the Settings icon in the lower-right corner of the window, and you'll see a check box for Favorites, Frequently logged in, Privacy Report, Siri Suggestions, Playlists, iCloud taps, and background image. You can also select wallpaper for the background, or you can select your own wallpaper using the big + button.

Configure the wallpaper tinting in Windows

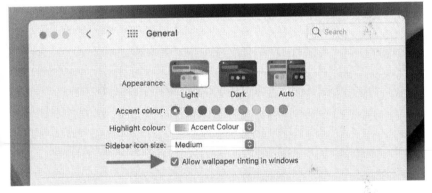

Although by default the MacOS Big Sur windows are tinted based on color of the wallpaper in the desktop, even though there is something between the wallpaper and the window.

You can disable the windows color tinting by going to Systems preference > General and untick the box beside **Allow wallpaper tinting in windows**.

Use battery health controls

In macOS Catalina 10.15.5, Apple introduced battery health management, which limits the charging of your battery of the MacBook to extend its life if it is often plugged into a power source.

Before that, it was not clear if the Mac's battery charging was limited, but in Big Sur, you can find this information in the battery menu bar item, and even force it to charge fully when you need it, using the **Charge to Full Now** option.

Keyboard shortcuts with reminders

There is a new keyboard shortcut in reminders that makes it easy to make changes, such as navigating the list and setting a specific date.

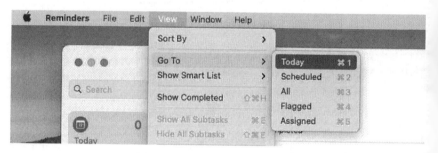

Personalize the control center

In System Preferences, the Dock & Menu Bar menu allows you to select what is available in the Control Center. You can activate or deactivate controls individually such as Wi-Fi, Bluetooth, AirDrop, DND, keyboard brightness, etc.

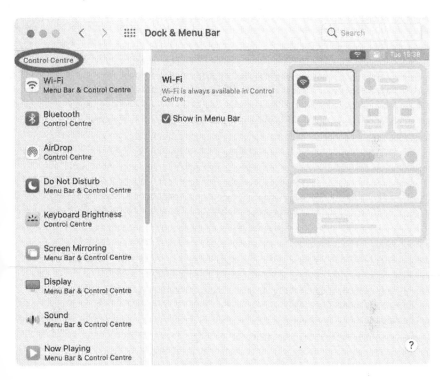

You can also find additional control centre models such as shortcut accessibility, battery, etc.

Pin the control centre option to the menu bar

Your favorites menu items in control center can be pinned at the top of the menu bar for easy access.

Just long click on an item in the control centre and drag it with your cursor to the menu bar.

Import passwords and settings from Chrome

Safari allows you to import passwords and settings from Google Chrome, including your history and bookmarks.

In the Safari menu bar, you can find a new setting under File>Import from>Google Chrome

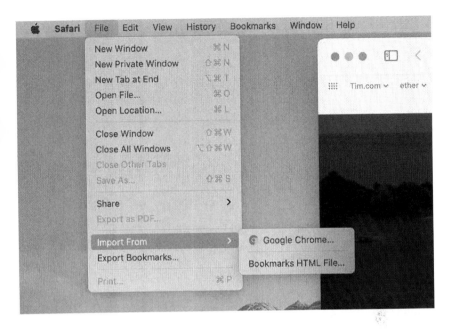

New wallpapers

Big Sur brings 40 new wallpapers to macOS, some of which may be familiar. Because most of them look at Apple's customized images in ios 14.2.

According to Big Sur, you can find more images of mountain and rock formations in System Preference> Desktop & Screen Saver, as well as pictures with different lighting conditions.

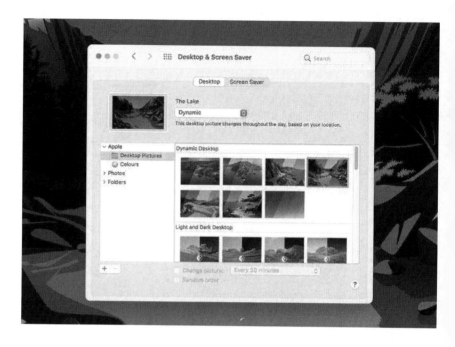

Made in the USA
Middletown, DE
27 June 2021